DRAW
Alien Fantasies

by

Damon J. Reinagle

SCHOLASTIC INC.
New York Toronto London Auckland Sydney

All my thanks and gratitude to Edgar Rice
Burroughs for his motivational novels, and
to Salvador Dali, Vincent Van Gogh and
Frank Frazetta, for their inspirational art.

–DJR

No part of this publication may be reproduced in whole or in part, or stored in a retrieval
system, or transmitted in any form or by any means, electronic, mechanical, photocopying,
recording, or otherwise, without written permission of the publisher. For information
regarding permission, write to Peel Productions, P.O. Box 546, Columbus, NC 28722.

ISBN 0-590-03741-2

12 11 10 9 8 7 6 5 4 3   8 9/9 0 1 2 3/0

Printed in the U.S.A.   40

First Scholastic printing, September 1998

Table of Contents

Before you begin...

Check your gauges, ready your booster rockets and fasten your safety harness for galactic drawing adventures! *Draw Alien Fantasies* will show you how. We begin with simple instructions, some common sense drawing rules and basic shapes. As we advance we will add details—textures, patterns and shading— as we put it all together.

It is important to begin at the beginning of this book and follow directions, one step at a time. If you do, you will be surprised at how easy it is to draw **great** Alien Fantasies. If, however, you skip ahead and attempt more advanced drawings, without following the beginning instructions, you may become a frustrated, unprepared artist. And, that's kind of like leaving Earth's orbit, and then realizing you've left your prepackaged food hundreds of miles below. So check your supplies, buckle up, be patient with yourself, and start from the beginning in order to be prepared for the drawing adventures ahead!

You will need:
- **pencil**
- **pencil sharpener**
- **eraser**
- **paper**
- **ruler**
- **a place to draw**
- **SUPER POSITIVE ATTITUDE!**

Let the adventures begin!

Common Sense Drawing Rules

Rule I

LOOK! See the shapes

Most everything you can draw is based on simple geometric shapes like circles, ovals, squares, rectangles and triangles. If you concentrate and observe, you can see shapes in everything you look at. *LOOK! See the shapes!*

Rule II

Sketch super lightly—always, always, always!

Reconstructive surgery (erasing) is much easier if you sketch lightly. And, light sketch lines help create form and texture in shapes. So always, always, always *sketch super lightly!*

Rule III

Be Creative! Use your imagination.

You could become an expert at copying the step by step drawings in this book. But, the real satisfaction comes when you make up your own characters and fantasy worlds, from your imagination. So *be creative! Use your imagination!*

Rule IV

Practice, Practice, Practice!

If at first you don't succeed...*practice, practice, practice* and you will get better.

Attention! ¡OJO! Achtung!

All galactic artists who follow the Common Sense Drawing Rules are guaranteed *GREAT* Alien Fantasy drawings.

Chapter 1 • Drawing Basics

Warm-Ups And Scribbles

Take some scrap paper and practice drawing circles, ovals and lines.

Warm-ups and scribbles loosen up your hand, arm and imagination.

Barely let your pencil tip touch the paper as you make the circular motions of varying sizes.

Scribble lines ever so lightly—draw some straight, curved, jagged, wavy, squiggly and wiggly.

Use your imagination. Make them up as you go.

Build the artist touch in your hands and make drawing become second nature—as easy as riding a bike! Try these warm-ups every day before you draw.

Practice every day!

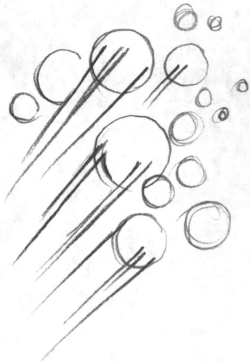

Cyclops

Let's draw our alien Cyclops buddy from page 7. It can easily be drawn from lots of spinning, space circles!

Step 1

Lightly sketch the circle and egg shape.

Step 2

Inside the egg shape, sketch an oval to form the eye.

Sketch three circles on each side of the body circle, to shape the arms.

At the bottom of the round belly, draw a small oval.

Step 3

Draw a small circle on each side of his head. Attach these to his head with a slightly curved antenna line.

Draw the eye. Add a big mouth and shape thick fingers, from the bottom arm circles.

Draw a few floating energy bubbles below his belly.

Step 4

Add details to the eye. Draw the tongue. Shape the arms and body.

Erase guide lines you no longer need.

Look at the cyclops in action on page 7. See how shading and a wild imagination add realism to our friendly floating friend!

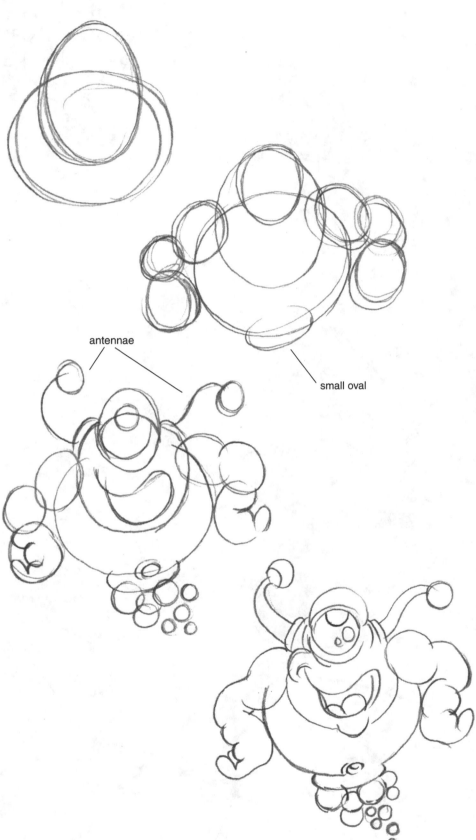

antennae

small oval

Tilting Ovals

Draw the SPP-7

Many drawings start with circles and ovals. See how this front view of a SPP (single passenger pod) shows a circle shape. Notice also how the wings point straight out.

If our pilot turns the pod, one way or another, to avoid an asteroid, the circle becomes a tilting oval, and we see a side view of the SPP.

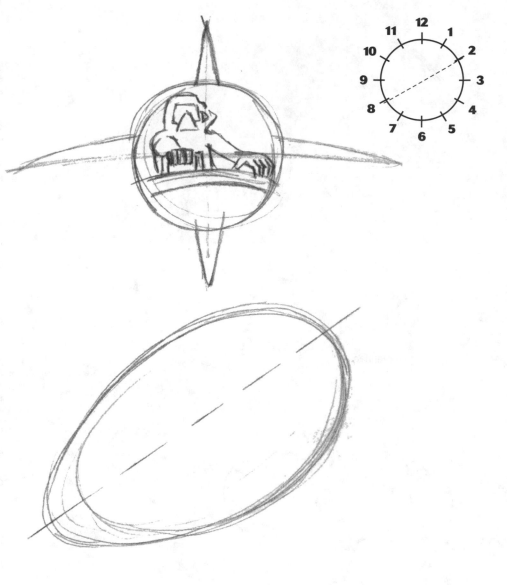

Step 1

Lets draw the SPP-7 in action. Notice how it tilts. Compare the tilt to the clock face above. The oval pod is tilting at an angle of about 2 o'clock and 8 o'clock. Draw the large tilting oval.

Step 2

Next add the curved triangle shapes of the wings.

Add a straight line to show where the wing connects to the side of the pod.

Draw two curved lines to shape the cockpit of the pod.

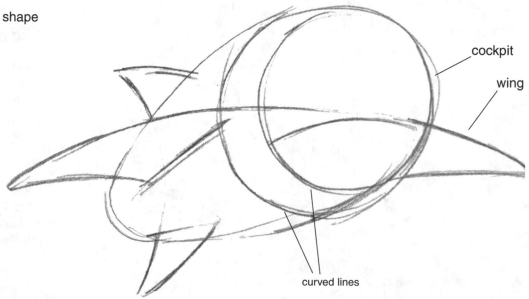

cockpit

wing

curved lines

Step 3

Look inside the cockpit. What basic shapes do you see?

Sketch the pilot with helmet, hands and the four headlamps.

Add additional lines to shape the wings and body of the SPP.

Clean up—erase any sketch lines you no longer need.

Step 4

Look closely at the shapes and shading in this drawing. See how each shape has been outlined and detailed. Notice the repeated pencil lines for shading.

Let's add the details. Shape and shade your drawing. Detail the pilot's helmet, body, arms and hands.

Don't forget the SPP-7 logo on the side of the pod.

Draw the triangle shaped blasts from the ship's rear rockets.

Add the distant asteroids we're soaring past.

Space Fact...

John H. Glenn, Jr. was the first American in orbit, circling the Earth three times in his space ship—the Friendship 7, reaching altitudes in excess of 250 km!

Space Question...

What is an asteroid?

Space Helmet

Whether you pilot a bike or a space ship, a protective helmet is very important gear. Let's draw a custom made one.

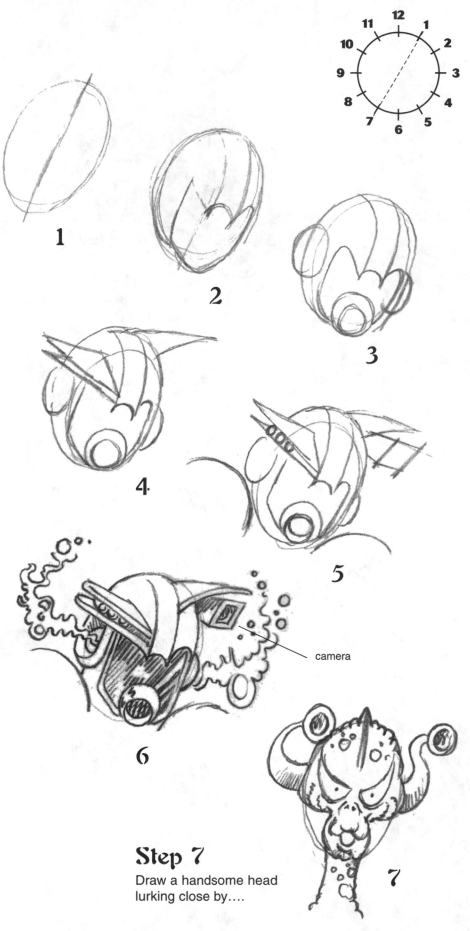

Step 1

Look at the clock face above. Sketch an oval, which tilts at the same angle, for the helmet.

Step 2

Look at the shape of the face shield. Sketch it. Add two curved lines to connect the face shield with the top of the helmet.

Step 3

Sketch an oval on the left side of the face, and a half oval on the right for the ear holes. Sketch two small circles—one inside the other—for the mouthpiece.

Step 4

Add triangular fins to the top and side of the helmet.

Step 5

Add three small lights between the side fins. Draw a square shape, on the right, for a camera. Add a line to shape the mouthpiece. Draw two curved lines for the round shoulders. Erase guide lines you no longer need.

Step 6

Look! See the shading, vapors oozing, thickened fins…. Add shading and the details.

camera

Step 7

Draw a handsome head lurking close by….

Chapter II • Rods And Joints

The Futurenaut

If all the metal space gear was removed from the futurenaut, on page 13, we would clearly see muscle and skin underneath. If we removed the muscle and skin, we would see the skeleton.

An artist always needs to know the way the skeleton bones and joints fit together. But, it's much easier to sketch basic shapes—RODS (lines) and JOINTS (ovals) to represent the skeleton.

LOOK carefully at the skeleton of our future space explorer.

Step 1

Let's begin by sketching an oval for the head, a triangle for the torso and a smaller triangle inside, for the pelvis.

Step 2

Next sketch the rods and joints for the shoulders, arms, hands, thighs, knees, and lower legs.

Step 3

Add lines for the neck. Sketch face lines for eye and mouth placement.

Outline and shape the arms and legs. Add ovals for the feet.

Erase guide lines you no longer need.

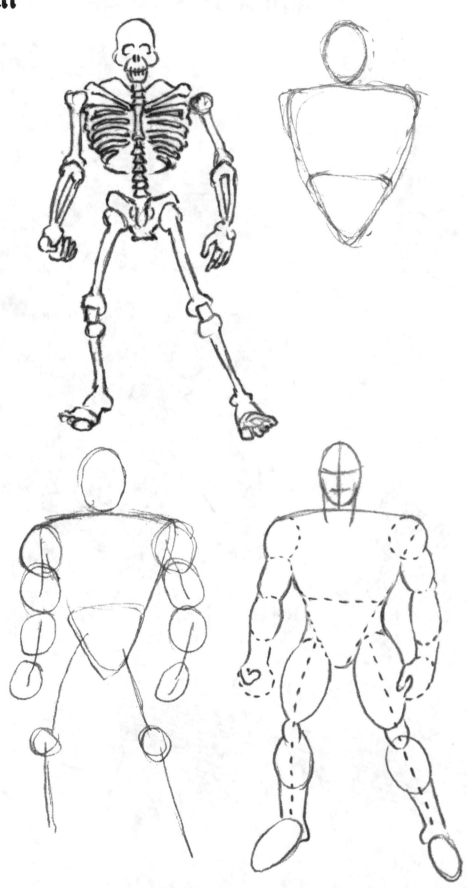

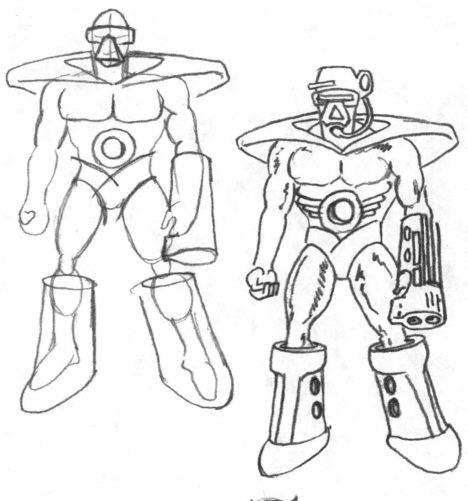

Step 4

Starting at the top, let's add the metal space gear.

Draw a rectangle and triangle for the helmet.

Sketch a wide power cape above the shoulders. Shape the broad chest. Draw a donut design on the stomach. Next add support bands across the pelvis.

Sketch the mechanical laser gauntlet over his left hand.

Sketch BIG boots over his calves and feet.

Clean up any smudges with your eraser.

Step 5

LOOK at this galactic hero carefully.

Shape, shade and outline each and every detail of your fine Futurenaut.

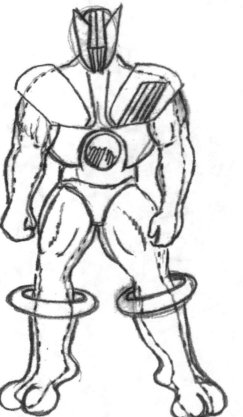

Artist Tip:

Once you know how to draw, using the rod and joint system, anything is possible!

By changing details, you can create a totally different character.

What details have I changed to come up with this cat-like character?

Floater

The Floater floats and flies freely, and is a fine example of how the rod and joint system works.

Step 1

LOOK at these floating ovals. Notice the angle of each one.

First, sketch the two head ovals. Next sketch the two upper body ovals—one inside the other. Lightly add a circle for the pelvis.

Step 2

LOOK at all those rods and joints, circles, and curved lines on this floater.

Sketch the antenna—two lines upward with circles on top.

Draw a circle and a half circle for the eyes.

Add the rods and joints for arms and hands. Notice the triangle shape on its left hand.

Connect the chest to the pelvis with curved lines.

Step 3

Add lines to thicken the antennae.

Add lines to thicken the arms. Look at the horn shaped hands! Shape these.

Add rods and joints to form the legs.

Erase guide lines you no longer need.

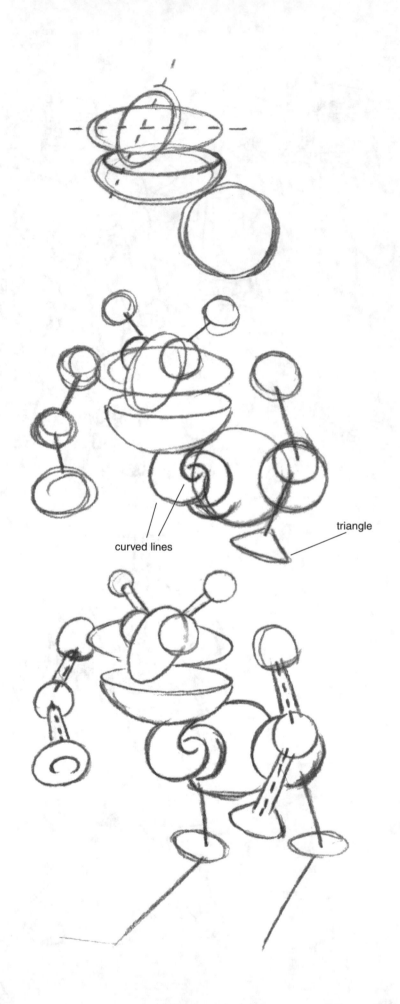

curved lines

triangle

Step 4

Draw the halo shaped rings around the antenna.

Add a slit in the left eye. Draw the round nostrils.

Draw lines to shape the upper and lower legs. Draw small ovals inside the knee ovals to create their halo shape.

Erase guide lines and clean up any smudges.

Step 5

Outline and add detail lines on arms and legs.

The Floater propels itself through space using compressed air jettisoned through its arms and legs. Draw a few lines to suggest this jet propulsion.

Artist Tip:

REMEMBER the warm-ups and scribbles you learned on page 10? Practice makes better, and that kind of loose, playful warmup helps with a drawing like this.

YOU ARE STILL PRACTICING EVERY DAY, before you draw, RIGHT?

RIGHT!

Space Station Constructor

A space station is a satellite that serves as a stopping place for spacecraft, and a work place for constructors.

Using its many appendages, the hard working constructor builds many space station sites.

Step 1

Let's start with the constructor's head and torso. Sketch the head oval. Sketch the upside-down heart shaped oval for the torso.

Step 2

Draw two almond shaped eyes. Add short lines for the nose and mouth.

Sketch five connecting circles, beneath the torso, to shape the midsection.

Step 3

The many appendages of the constructor are formed using the familiar rod and joint system. Starting at the shoulders, sketch the ovals (joints) and lines (rods) to create arms.

Sketch a large oval, at the base of the midsection, for the pelvis. Add lines and ovals to form legs.

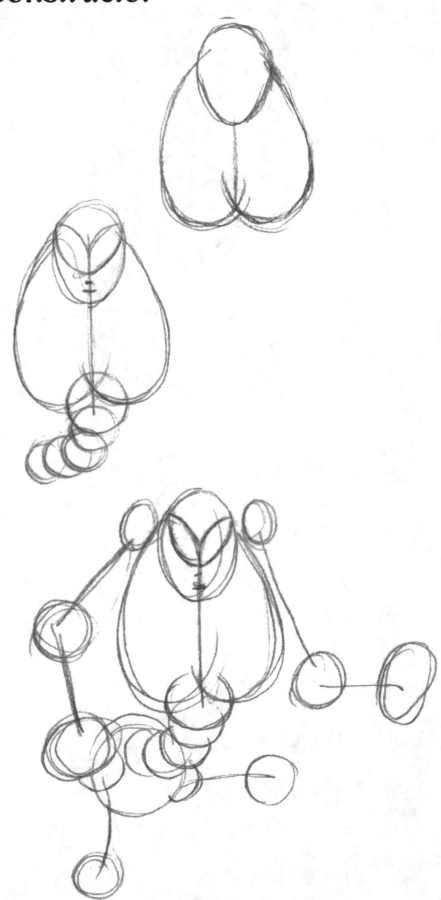

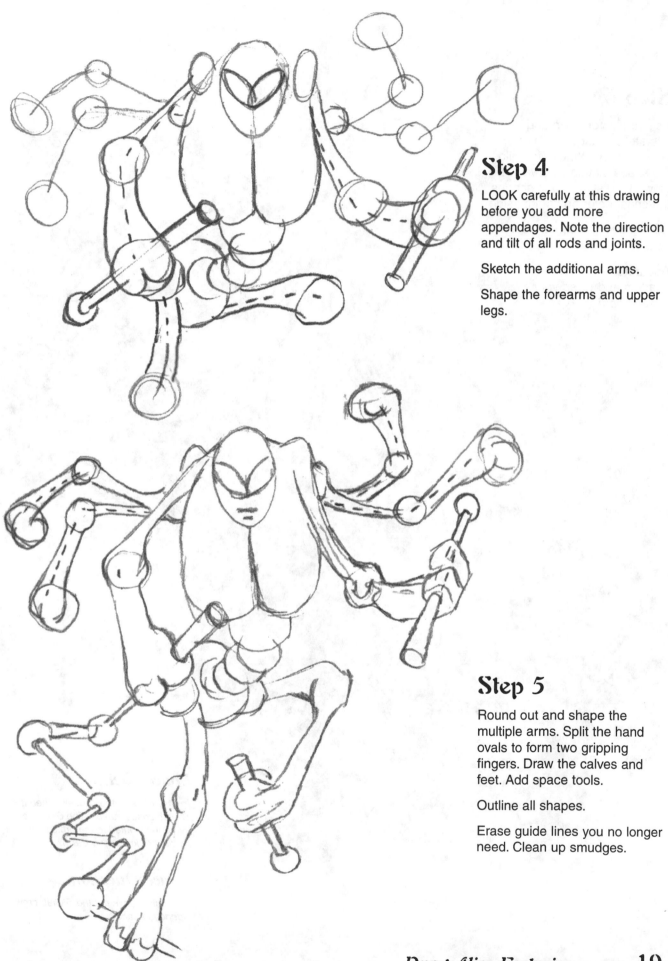

Step 4

LOOK carefully at this drawing before you add more appendages. Note the direction and tilt of all rods and joints.

Sketch the additional arms.

Shape the forearms and upper legs.

Step 5

Round out and shape the multiple arms. Split the hand ovals to form two gripping fingers. Draw the calves and feet. Add space tools.

Outline all shapes.

Erase guide lines you no longer need. Clean up smudges.

Step 6

As star clusters twirl and interstellar dust swirls, the constructor continues to build the space station walkway. The glow of a distant moon shades the constructor on its right side.

LOOK! See the constructor in action.

Add details—stars, dust, shading and...*use your imagination!*

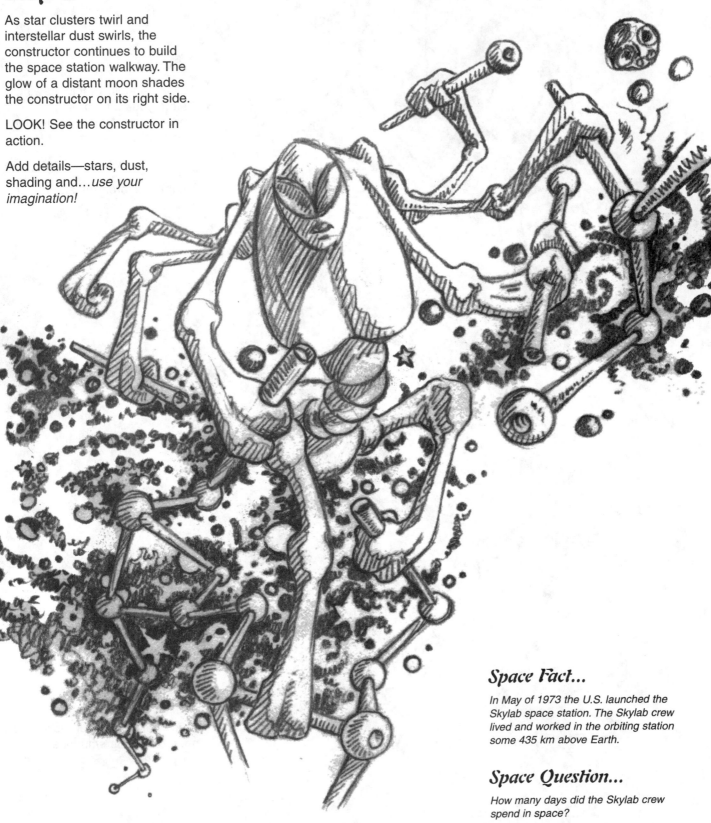

Space Fact...

In May of 1973 the U.S. launched the Skylab space station. The Skylab crew lived and worked in the orbiting station some 435 km above Earth.

Space Question...

How many days did the Skylab crew spend in space?

Space Cow

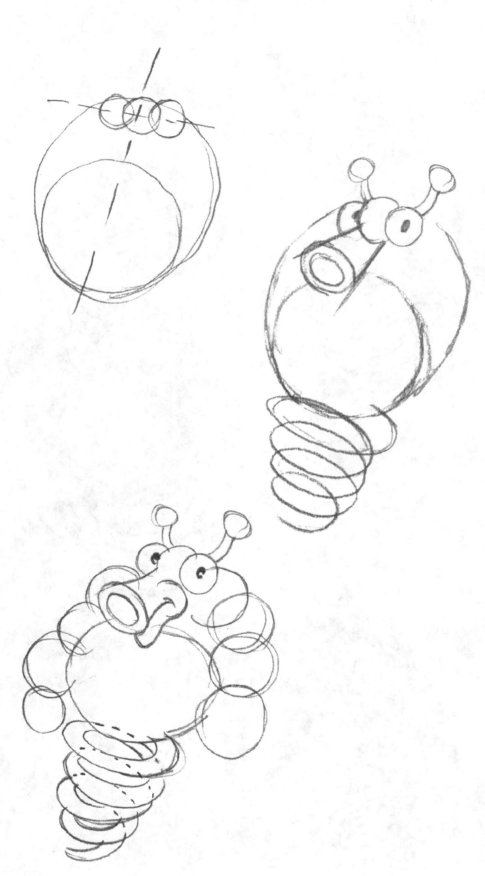

Attention! ¡OJO! Achtung!

Space cow alert! Space cow approaching at a1 o'clock/7 o'clock tilt.

In deep space you never know who or what you might come across. Let's capture this space cow on our radar screen and drawing board.

Step 1

Start by sketching a large circle for the body. Sketch another smaller circle inside, near the bottom, for the stomach. Lightly add three smaller circles, in a line across the top of the body circle, for the eyes and forehead.

Step 2

Add horns—lines and circles. Draw pupils in the eyes. Sketch the cone shape snout of the Space Cow—two ovals and two lines.

The Cow springs through space on a bouncy spiral springie-sprongie. Draw her long spiral spring—about four loops long. CONCENTRATE— you can do it!

Step 3

Draw curved lines to shape the Space Cow's jaw and lower lip. Reshape the snout to curve slightly on the top and bottom.

Sketch four ovals on each side of the body, to form the bovine arms. Add curved lines to shape the springie-sprongie.

Erase guide lines you no longer need.

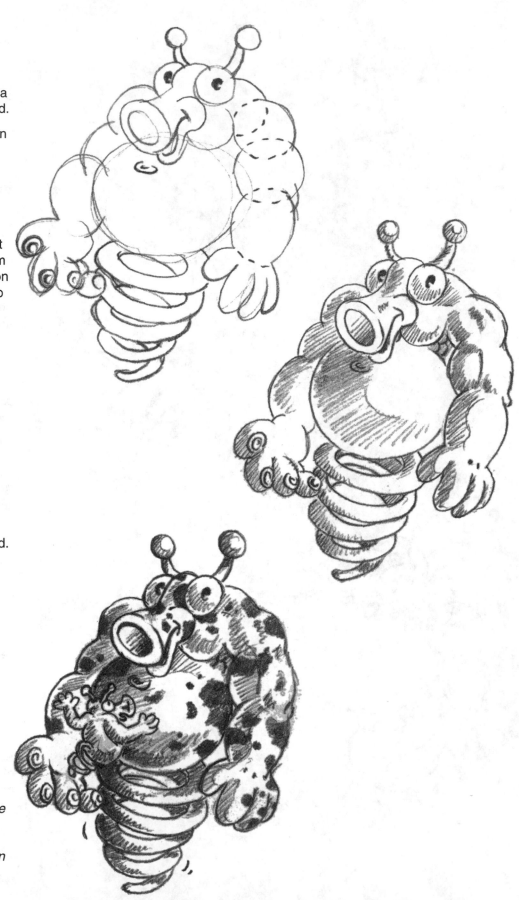

Step 4

Outline and shape the arms. Add three chubby fingers and a thumb, of course, to each hand.

Draw the small round shape on the belly.

Erase guide lines.

Step 5

Imagine a strong beam of light shining down, on the cow, from the upper right. Add shading on the opposite side of the cow to show shadows of the light source.

Step 6

LOOK! See the details in this finished drawing—the suction cup finger tips…a bouncing baby Space Cow? What other details do you see?

Draw them. Shade the dark cow spots.

Clean up smudges. Erase guide lines you no longer need.

Artist Tip:

Always use a clean piece of paper to cover the shaded areas you've completed. There is less chance of smudging a drawing if you cover the finished areas, as you work on other details of the drawing.

Chapter III • Heroes & Villains

Variety In Space

Variety is the SPICE of life in space, where creatures roam in all sorts of sizes and shapes. In this vast unexplored territory, the sky is the limit. So-o-o-o use your imagination. Create any creature you wish, including characters inspired by basic geometric shapes like these. Good Luck! Let your creativity take you to other galaxies and beyond!

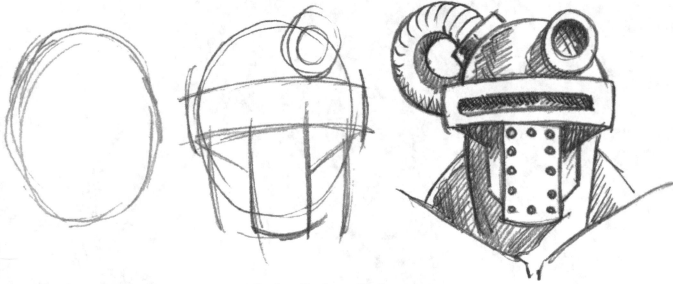

All three of these characters are created using the basic shapes—circles, ovals, squares and rectangles. Explore with these examples, then invent your own characters!

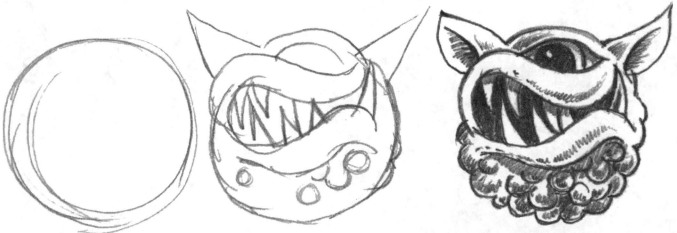

Small Saucer Guy

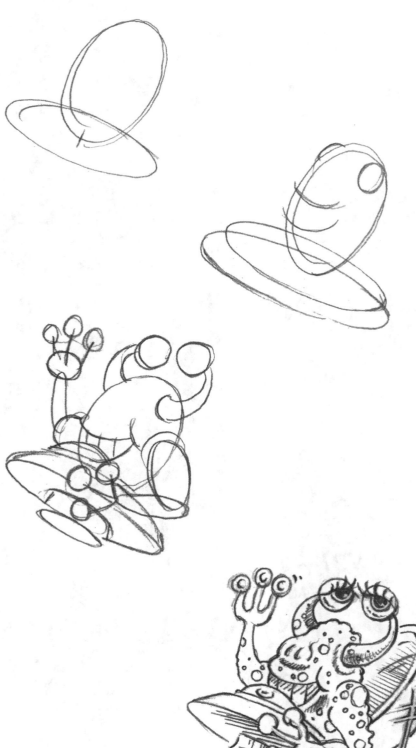

Remember this character from page 6? He's got a face that only a grandparent could love. Well, maybe another saucer could love him too.

Step 1

Sketch a light tilted oval for his head. Sketch another oval, horizontally tilted, for his body.

Step 2

Add a small half-circle on the left side of the head and a small circle on the right side of the head—for horn holders.

Sketch curved lines to hold that big mouth.

Sketch another, horizontally tilted oval, for his saucer base.

Step 3

Draw the horns. Shape the mouth and teeth.

Using the rod and joint system, sketch ovals and lines to form arms and three fingered hands.

Draw ovals and lines to shape the saucer base.

Step 4

Add a few more details and this guy will be the life of any tea party.

Outline and shape the warty, wrinkled head and body. Shade his pitch fork fingers. Detail his eyes. Add a bubble canopy for his saucer top. Add shading, shadows and fuel for take off.

Cyborg Patrol

If anyone can keep the peace in deep space, it's this CP Officer! As they say in Cyborg, "Don't mess with an armed robot."

Step 1

Sketch a large oval, for the body. Sketch a much smaller oval on top, for the head. Connect the two ovals with a short neck line. Sketch lines for arms.

Sketch two long ovals, below the body, for the patrol's thighs. Sketch long "J"shaped lines, under the leg ovals, for the calves and feet.

Step 2

See the strange wing-like structures on the patrol's shoulders? These house the patrol lights. Sketch these. Add a line and oval for the neck.

Sketch an oval and two curved lines to form chest armor. Look, then shape the thighs and calves.

Erase guide lines you no longer need.

Step 3

Outline and shape the light mounts. Add tear-drop shaped shoulder pads under the mounts. Draw additional lines to shape the arms.

Add two curved lines, under the CP's left arm.

Look at those metallic legs! Add lines and ovals to shape these.

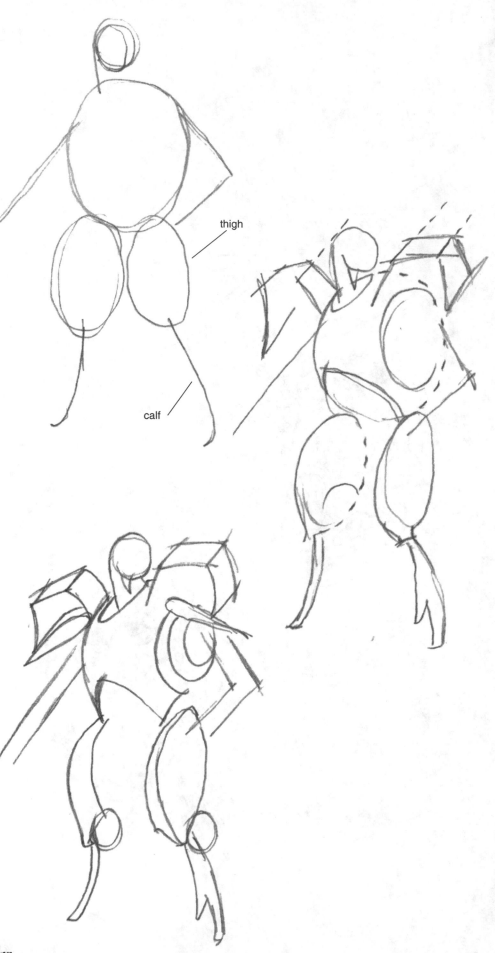

thigh

calf

Step 4

Add lines for a mounted light and a square helmet to arm this CP's head.

Add additional lines to shape and thicken the shoulder pads.

Look at the shape of the Cyborg's powerful arms! Shape them by adding curved and straight lines, with laser mounts on the tips.

Draw a spool shape to form the pelvis.

Add lines and ovals to the leg armor. Don't forget the triangle shaped club feet.

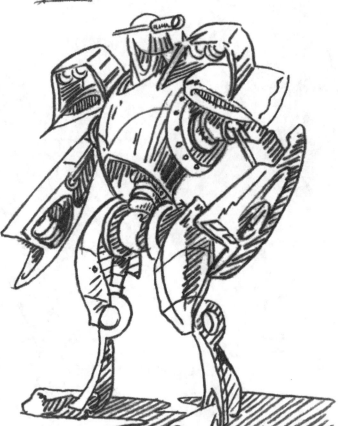

Step 5

Our shining Cyborg hero stands its solitary post ready to answer any distress call.

Study the details—lights in the lamp mounts (circles within circles), the way the spool-like pelvis connects to the torso, the contrast of light and dark, shapes and the shadows they cast.

Use your imagination, as you detail and shade your drawing of the CP.

Great job!

Pirate Extraordinaire

This extraordinary pirate has energy to spare. Watch out for the harmless-looking vapor energy she holds!

Step 1

Sketch an oval for the head, a larger oval for the upper body, and a curved "V" shape for the lower body.

Step 2

Look carefully at these spider-like lines. See the shapes and how they connect. Lightly sketch these connecting lines.

Step 3

Sketch a small diamond and an upside-down teardrop shape, on top of her head. Sketch curved lines, on each side of her head, to form hair.

Add another half-circle, inside the first one, to shape the shoulder guards. Add lines to shape the chest strap.

Sketch rods and joints to form legs and feet.

Step 4

Add a curved line, on each side of the teardrop, to start the headdress. Add the eyes, nostrils and mouth. Sketch two half-circles for round shoulders.

Sketch rods and joints for arms and hands. Draw lines to complete the protective body garments. Shape the upper legs and boots. Sketch lines and an oval, in her right hand, for a laser shooter!

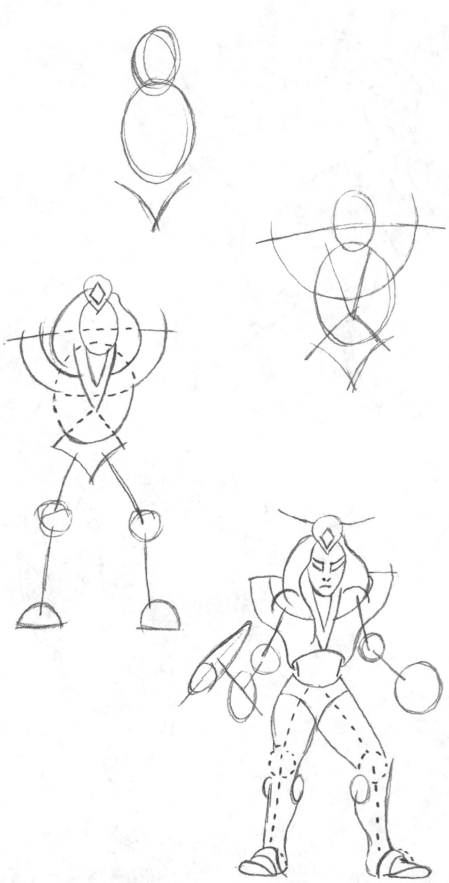

Step 5

Look at the skull headdress and how it flows into her thick head of hair. Draw lines to shape her headdress and hair.

Detail the eyes and mouth.

Notice her muscular arms and the zigzag lines for fingers, on her left hand. These will hold lightning, while the fingers on her right hand will control the laser shooter.

Shape her arms and gloves. Add lines to shape the laser shooter.

Outline and shape her boots.

Clean up—erase guide lines you no longer need.

Step 6

Look!

Now, add shading, shadows and details. Use wiggly, squiggly lines to form the vapor energy she holds in her left hand.

Use your imagination to design a laser shooter.

Artist Tip:

To add life to this pirate's eyes, darken them, but leave a small white dot as a highlight.

Mercurian Guard

The palace of the Royal Planet of Mercury is protected by an army of these regal creatures.

Step 1

See the tilt of these two ovals.

Sketch them—a small one for the head, and a larger one for the body.

Step 2

Lightly sketch shoulder ovals. Sketch a curved line connecting the top of the head with the guard's left shoulder.

Sketch another curved line to divide the torso.

Step 3

Add ovals for eyes. Sketch a curved line to shape the face.

Look at the curved body sections. Draw lines to section the chest and stomach.

Sketch lines to shape the long insect-like thighs. Sketch ovals for knees. Sketch rods and joints for calves and feet.

Look at the moon shape of the tail. Add the tail.

Step 4

Look at the sections of this thick head and neck. Add these. Add feelers to the mouth.

Sketch rods and joints for the arms.

Draw lines to section the tail. Add more sections to thicken the lower back.

Add lines to shape the calves and feet.

Erase guide lines you no longer need.

Step 5

Starting at the top, study the insect shape and details. See how outlining and shading makes the guard look lifelike.

Outline, shape, detail and shade this regal creature. Remember to add the antennae and spear.

Marvelous Mercurian Guard!

Astronaut Explorer

Drawing an astronaut in action is easy, if you look at the shapes, sketch super lightly, use your imagination and practice drawing.

Step 1

Our astronaut drawing begins with three simple shapes—a circle for the helmet, a long oval for the shoulders, and a diamond shape (that looks like home plate on a baseball field) for the body.

Lightly sketch these three shapes.

Step 2

Sketch the rectangle box shape, on the explorer's shoulders, to form the Portable Life Support System (PLSS).

Sketch two smaller circles, within the helmet, for a visor shield.

Using the rod and joint system, sketch the ovals and lines to form the arms and legs.

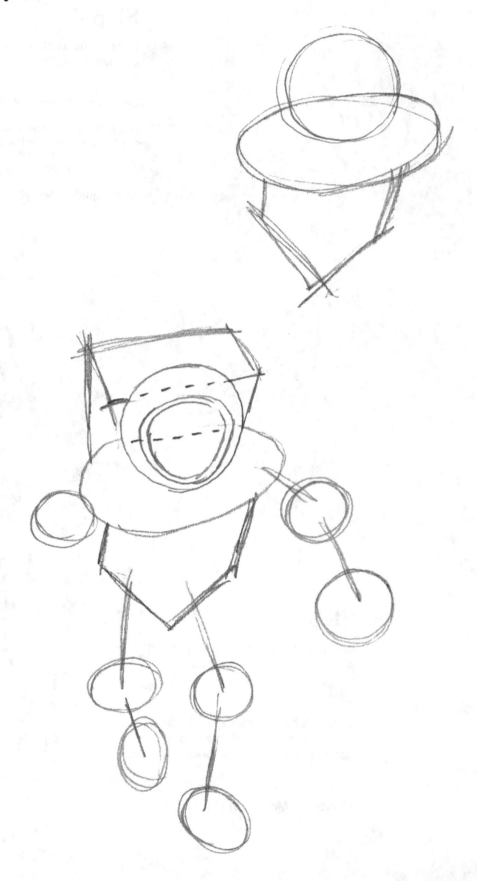

Step 3

Starting at the top, shape the PLSS unit. Sketch a starburst reflection on the visor shield.

Sketch a rectangle, for a flag, on the astronaut's left shoulder. Outline and shape the arm and glove—make fingers and thumb curve inward to hold on to a stalagmite. The astronaut's right hand is reaching out to hoist the American flag. Shape this glove with out-stretched fingers and a thumb.

Add a rectangle, on the chest, and an oxygen hose for air.

Shape and outline the legs.

Erase guide lines you no longer need.

Step 4

Add the oxygen hose above the astronaut's right shoulder. Shade the visor.

Add lines to detail the space suit, gloves and boots.

Using page 23 as your guide, add shading, and a rocky terrain. Don't forget the flag.

oxygen hose

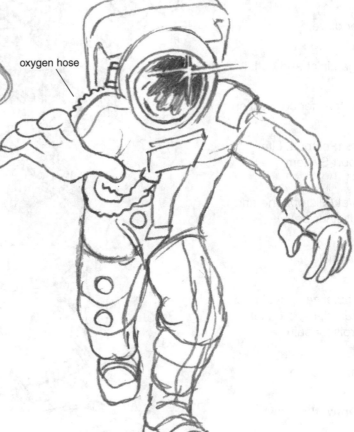

Space Fact...

Neil Armstrong and Edwin Aldrin, Jr. took the first steps on the moon's surface in July of 1969.

Space Question...

Which astronaut was orbiting the moon, in Apollo 11's command module, during the eight day mission?

Basic Astronaut Spacesuit

Spacesuits are designed to protect astronauts from the environment of space—radiation, heat, cold and pieces of debris called micrometeors. A spacesuit is also designed so that it's easy to move around in.

Knowing the basic parts of the spacesuit, and placement of each part, will help you in proportioning and drawing an astronaut better.

To help you learn the parts and their placement, study this spacesuit—top to bottom.

A - Oxygen tube

B - Sleeve pocket

C - Metal connecting ring

D - Outer glove

E - Oxygen inlet and outlet

F - Urine transfer connection

G - PLSS (Personal Life Support System

H - Helmet (Microphone and headset inside)

I - Visor shield

J - Computerized chest pack (Water inlet and outlet controls for suit)

K - Outer overshoe

NOW... Draw it!

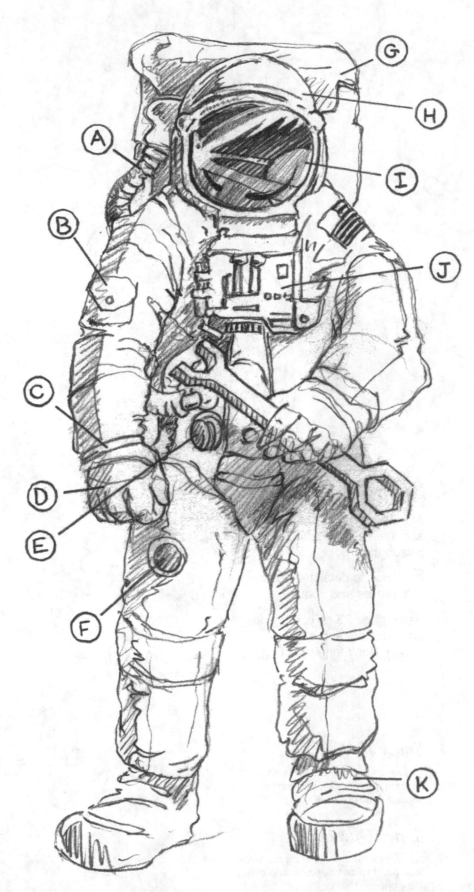

Chapter IV • Galactic Vehicles

Solo Land Explorer

Once on the surface of another planet, a space explorer needs a comfortable way to move around. The self-propelled Solo Land Explorer is the perfect solution!

Step 1

Sketch a long tilted oval with a circle a line inside for the cockpit area. Sketch another oval at the bottom for the grill.

Step 2

Sketch two horizontal ovals, for headlamps. Sketch a long triangle, at the back of the right headlamp. Add two circles, on the bottom, for leg joints.

Step 3

Add two curved lines to form the bubble shield. Draw a large reverse "S" on the side of the body unit. Add curves to the headlamps. Draw a circle and a curved line inside the right joint. Sketch rods and joints to form the legs.

Step 4

Sketch two half circles, in the cockpit—one for a helmet and one for the explorer's hands. Add curved lines to the back of the cockpit.

Draw the suspension arms, below the reverse "S". Add depth to the headlamps by drawing inside lines for lamps. Add lines to the grill opening and two curved lines for the left leg joint.

Outline and shape the legs and the boots.

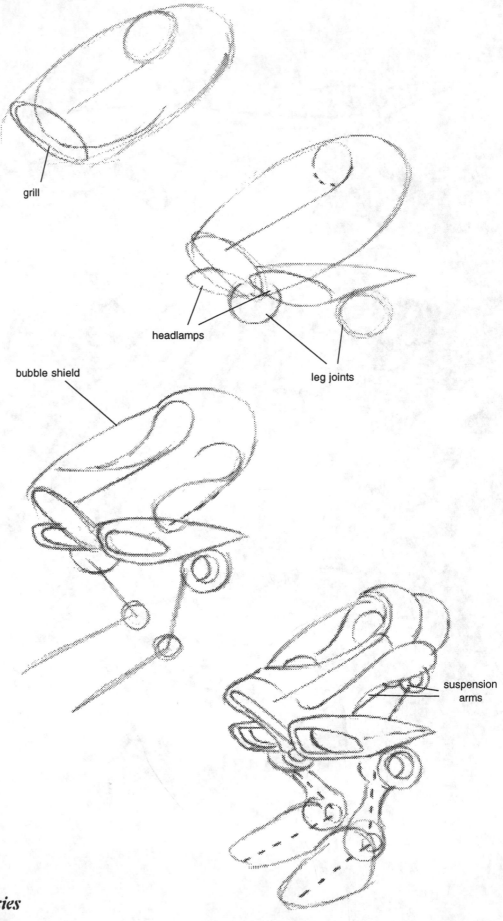

grill

headlamps

bubble shield

leg joints

suspension arms

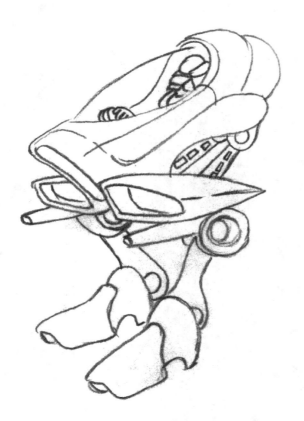

Step 5

Erase guide lines you no longer need.

Study the explorer's helmet—see how it is made up of many small shapes. Draw them. Draw fingers on the hand shape. Detail the suspension arms. Add a laser torch under each headlamp.

These boots are made for walking! Outline and shape the two sectioned walking boots.

Step 6

Let's give the explorer some company on this expedition. Study this detailed scene carefully. See the depth created by distant mountains and ridges. See the different sizes and positions of the other explorers. Give it a try—one line at a time. Add details and shading to finish your drawing.

Puddle Jumper for Two

Step 1

Sketch a half oval for the bubble top of this two person space craft. Draw two parallel lines (slightly curved in the middle) under the bubble top.

Step 2

Sketch two more, slightly curved, lines below the first two to shape the ship's middle section.

Draw a three-sided box shape for the base. Add another smaller box shape, under it, for the booster rocket.

Step 3

Sketch a curved line to shape the ends of the ship's middle sections.

Look at the triangle shapes on both sides of the base. They help the Puddle Jumper jump and land safely. See where they connect to the base and bottom of the mid-section? Sketch these triangles—three on each side.

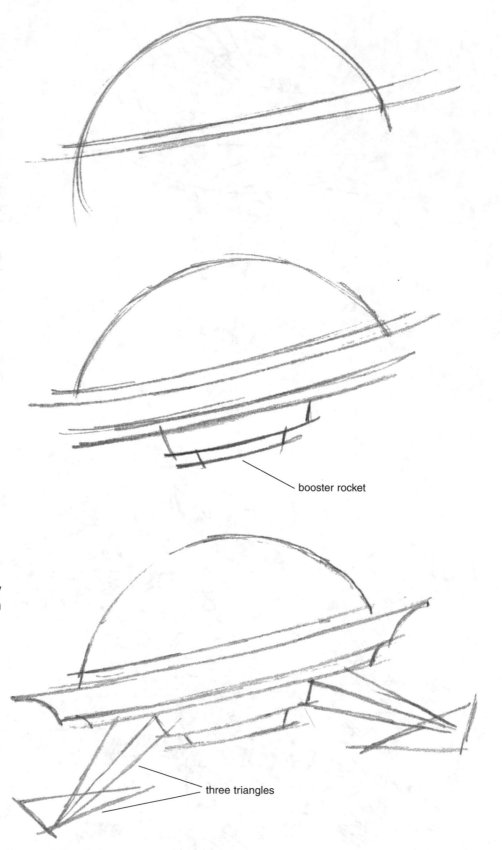

booster rocket

three triangles

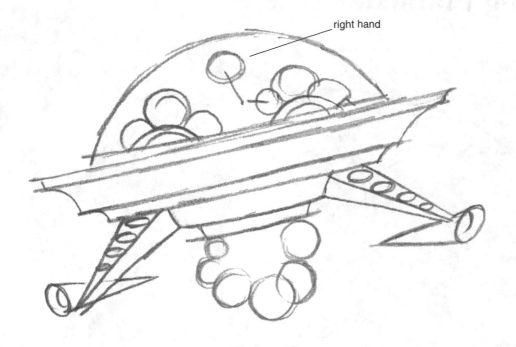

right hand

Step 4

Let's put the astronauts behind the controls, inside the cockpit bubble.

First draw the two steering wheels—two curved lines on each side. Look at the circles forming the astronauts' torsos. Notice the astronaut on your right has his right hand up. Sketch the circles and lines to shape the torsos.

Look at the the landing legs. Add ovals and lines to shape and detail these.

Directly under the space craft, sketch six small, connecting circles—to begin the rocket fuel blast.

Erase guide lines you no longer need.

Step 5

Now for the details that add life and excitement to the final drawing…such as…

…the astronaut's hands and helmets, the landing lights, the rocket blast, the shining, shaded bubble—and the starburst!

Outline, shade and detail your puddle jumper. Clean up any smudges.

¡Perfecto! Perfekt!

The Boomerang Marauder

This sleek speedster could get you from Earth to Alpha Centuri, and back, in no time flat!

Step 1

Look at these shapes. See where they overlap.

Sketch a flattened oval. Next, sketch a boomerang shape for the wings. Add two curved lines.

Step 2

See the half circle and triangle forming the speedster's front end? Add these.

Draw two curved lines—one on each side of the middle lines.

Erase any guide lines you no longer need.

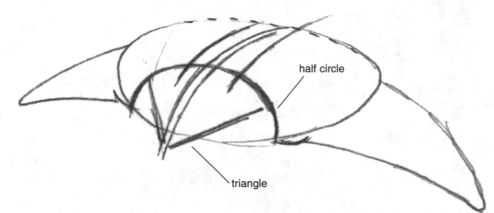

half circle

triangle

Step 3

Add curved lines, inside the original oval, to form the rim around the ship's middle.

Draw two more curved lines, to shape the rocket boosters.

Refine the shape of the front triangle. Outline and reshape the front end.

Erase guide lines you no longer need.

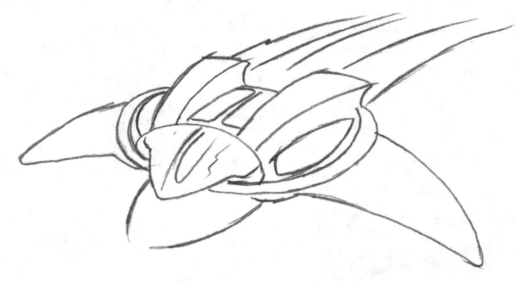

Step 4

Form the rocket boosters by adding a straight and curved line to the back end of each.

Draw lines, shooting out, to form the beginnings of the fuel explosions.

Sketch two curved lines, coming from the front of the vehicle, to form the laser guns.

Look! Do you see any other details added to this drawing?

Add them.

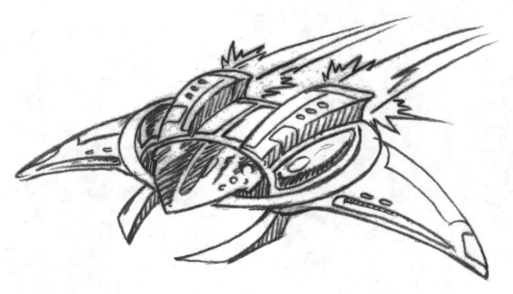

Step 5

Draw lines to finish the laser guns.

Shape, shade and outline this mean machine. Add details.

Make that fuel explode with zig-zag, squiggly lines.

This Marauder is moving on.

The Laser Scorpion

Whether using its lasers for constructing cities or defending them, this Scorpion really packs a sting!

Step 1

Sketch an oval with five lines across its width.

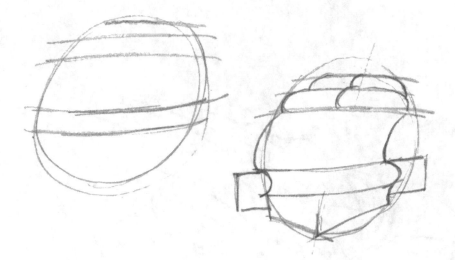

Step 2

See the separate sections of the Scorpion's body?

Using the oval as your guide, add curved lines to section and shape the body. Near the bottom, add a box shape on each side, to form spools for the lasers. Square off and reshape the bottom of the oval.

Erase guide lines you no longer need.

Step 3

Sketch an oval to form the cockpit. Draw small circles and long curved lines, to begin the beck legs.

Add curved lines, to shape the laser spools.

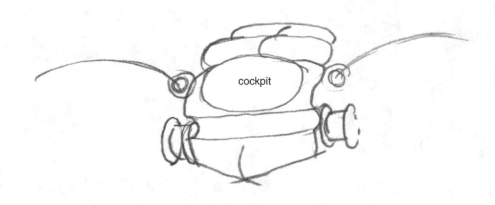

Step 4

Add three small rounded sections, to the back of the body, to form the Scorpion's tail.

Look carefully at the leg shapes and angles. Sketch additional curved and straight lines—starting from the small circles outside the cockpit—to form the rear legs and laser mounts.

Add lines to form the front legs.

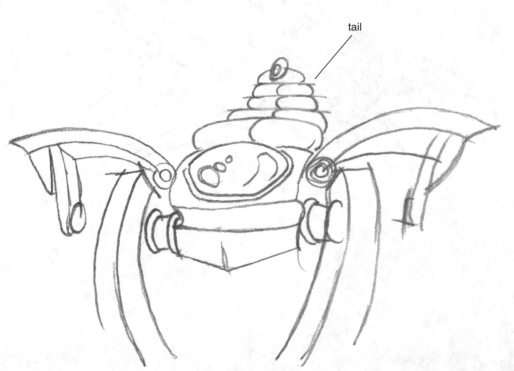

Step 5

Look! More legs and feet! See the various shapes—triangles, rectangles, ovals and diamonds. Add them to your drawing.

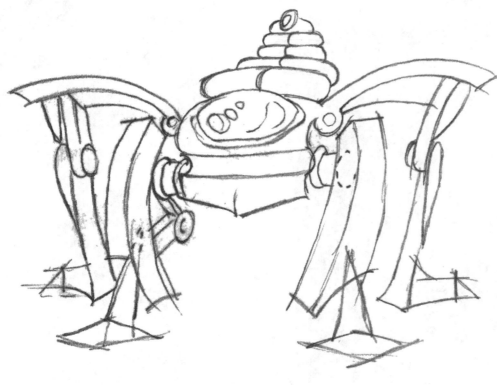

Step 6

Now for the details that add ZAP! and realism to this Scorpion.

Draw the long neon light shapes in the grill area.

Draw the needle point lasers.

Outline and shape the legs and feet.

Anything missing?

Feel free to make laser blast noises as you draw!

ZAP! Zzzzz! ZAP!

Space Fact...

In November of 1957, the U.S.S.R. launched Sputnik 2. LAIKA the dog was aboard. His seven day orbit proved that living creatures can survive in outer space!

Space Question...

What does the Russian word Sputnik mean?

Space Station Venus

Step 1

Lightly sketch a tilting oval. In the center sketch a smaller oval—approximately the size of the Venution Dractona coin. This should look like a floating donut!

Sketch two lines, crossing at the top right side of the coin shape—forming a large "X."

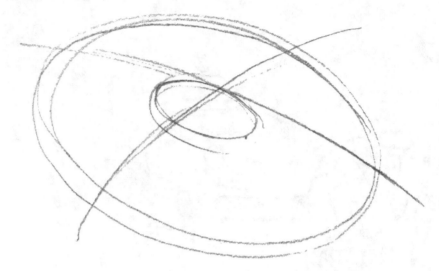

Step 2

Inside the Venution Dracton oval, sketch two more smaller ovals.

Add a straight line below each curved line—these spoke shapes are the beginnings of the space station's covered walkways.

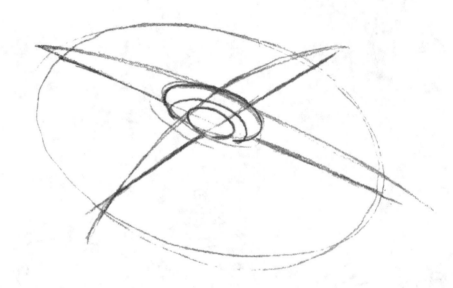

Step 3

See how the spoke shapes connect to the ship's hub.

Using the original curved lines as your guide, draw the curved lines connecting and covering the walkways from the ship's hub to stations 1, 2, 3 and 4.

Erase guide lines you no longer need.

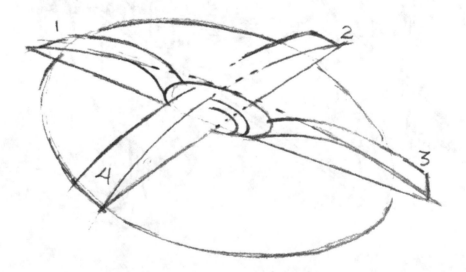

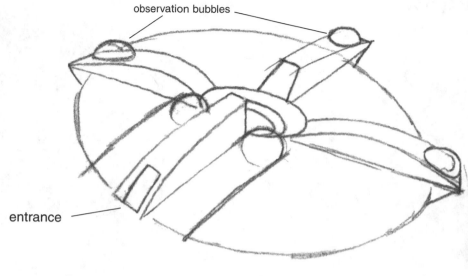

observation bubbles

entrance

Step 4

Draw small observation bubbles on top of stations 1, 2 and 3.

Sketch a rectangle for the outside entrance to station 4. Add lines and circles, on either side of walkway 4, to shape power boosters.

At the hub, draw lines to shape the entrances from the hub to stations 2 and 4.

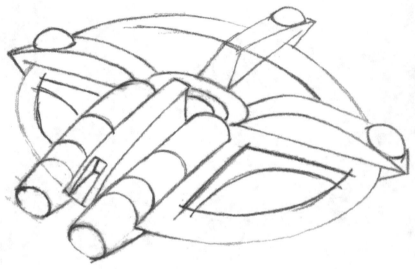

Step 5

Shape the power boosters—round the ends and add three curved lines.

Look at the entrance—see the lines added to create depth. Draw them.

Stop and look at the final drawing in Step 6. See the open areas, and window sections.

Let's sketch these sections now. First, draw the curved line across, and on both sides of station 2. Add lines—straight and curved—to shape the panel and open sections, to the left and right of the power boosters.

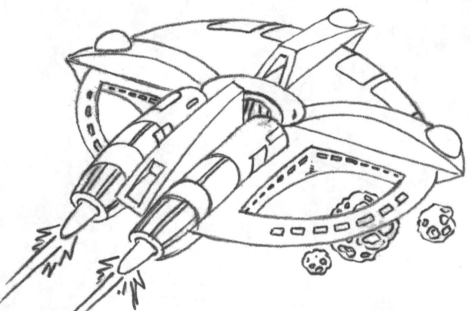

Step 6

Look at Space Station Venus majestically gliding above the tumbling meteorites.

Add the details—windows and more windows, panels and doors on the power boosters, ignition blasts, and any other details you wish to create.

Clean up any smudges with your eraser.

Deep Space Viper

The Deep Space Viper can be viewed in all its glory on page 35. Before you begin your drawing, study the Viper in action.

Step 1

Sketch a long teardrop shaped fuselage ending with an oval.

Step 2

Sketch another smaller oval over lapping the first. Sketch two triangles—one on each side of the fuselage. Sketch an oval at the base of the left triangle.

Step 3

Add the teardrop shape cockpit. Sketch four ovals, to start the power boosters. Round out and shape the wing and body lines.

Erase guide lines you no longer need.

Step 4

Look at the additional parts added in Step 4—lines to shape the power boosters, two wings, a rear cockpit bubble with two support struts (to hold the bubble in place), and lines to connect and shape the main exhaust port. Add these details.

Step 5

Detail and shade your Space Viper, using the drawing on page 35 as your guide.

Don't forget the jet fuel trail. Enjoy drawing as you blast off to deep space adventures!

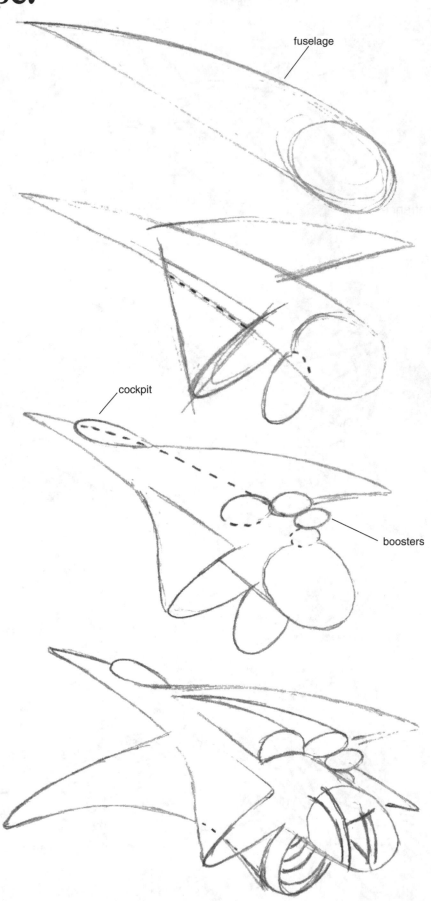

fuselage

cockpit

boosters

Overlapping

Creating depth in space is easy if you make some things look closer and some things look farther away. This is called overlapping.

Step 1

Sketch a distant—squiggly line—mountain range.

Step 2

In front of this mountain range, sketch another mountain range, and other strange mountain shapes.

Step 3

Add donut shapes for craters. Shade the distant mountains with diagonal lines.

Step 3

Add slightly darker diagonal lines to shade the second mountain range. Outline the crater rims with curly lines to make them appear lumpy. Sketch ovals to begin the emerging crater creature's eyes.

Step 4

Look! See the shading and shadows. The creature rises, and so does the moon. Outline and shape the craters. Draw wavy lines to create the wild creature's hair-do! Add the moon. Erase guide lines you no longer need. **Looking good!** *Name that creature!*

Space Shuttle

A space shuttle is a rocket plane that can be used many times. Rockets, filled with fuel, help it take off from earth.

Look carefully at the first sketch of the space shuttle. It consists of three ovals and four lines— All the lines start at one point, at the bottom, and connect to the ovals on top.

Step 1

Lightly sketch a large tilted oval and two smaller ovals—one on each side. Mark an "X" in the lower left corner of your drawing paper to show the one point where all lines start.

Use a ruler to line the "X" mark up with the outside of the small top oval. Draw line one. Move the top of the ruler, to line the "X" up with the outside edge of the large oval. Draw line two. Draw line three, between the point and the bottom side of the large oval. Draw line four from the point to the outside of the bottom oval.

Step 2

Sketch an egg shaped oval over the center of line two. Sketch a circle over the oval. Add another smaller circle. These will help shape the shuttle fuselage—body of the spacecraft.

Step 3

Look at the fuselage shape. Connect the oval and circles with three lines—slanting toward the one point. Draw two triangles for wings—a small one on top and a larger one on the bottom. Sketch a triangle on the top rear for a stabilizer.

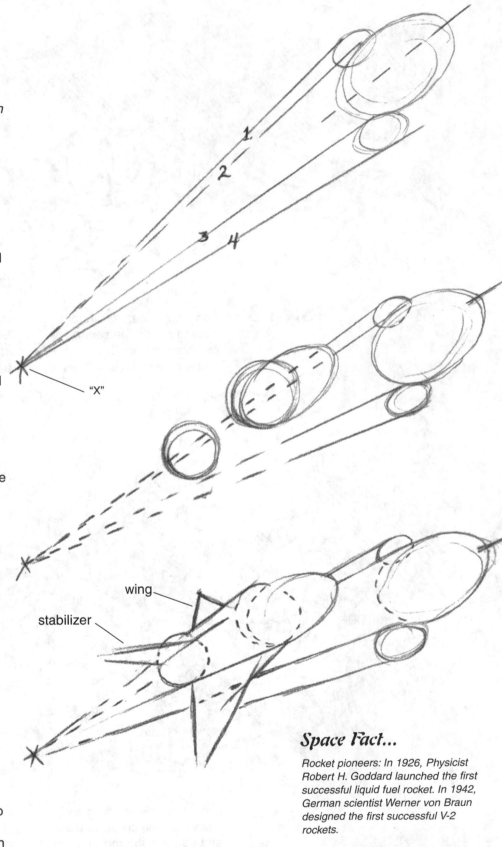

Space Fact...

Rocket pioneers: In 1926, Physicist Robert H. Goddard launched the first successful liquid fuel rocket. In 1942, German scientist Werner von Braun designed the first successful V-2 rockets.

Space Question...

What is a booster rocket?

Step 4

Erase any guide lines you no longer need.

Outline and trim the wing tips and the stabilizer. Sketch small ovals for rockets, on either side of the stabilizer. Sketch two curved lines, on the top front of the spacecraft, to shape the cockpit and window area. Add a small oval to the tip of the shuttle.

Draw squiggly lines, at the rear of the shuttle, to show the rocket fuel fumes.

How are you doing? The hard part is over—the basic shape of the shuttle is complete.

Step 5

Add lines to shape the spacecraft—body, wings, stabilizer, cockpit, windows and the USA insignia.

Add more exhaust fumes and curved dotted lines —in all directions, to show the ignition blast.

Step 6

Look! See the detailed shading, and the explosive ignition blast! Add these details.

Super shuttle!

Space Station Interior

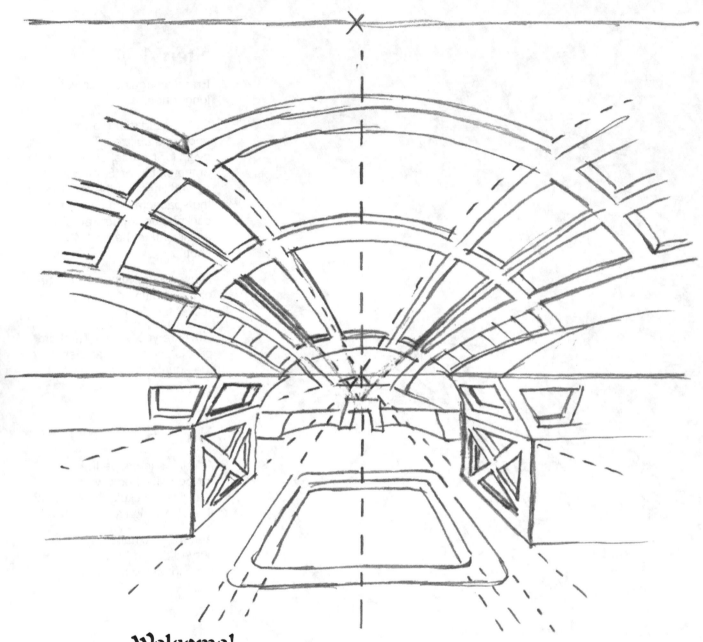

Welcome!
Willkommen! ¡Bienvenidos!

...to Space Station 2018.

Study this drawing. Like the space shuttle, it is drawn using one point perspective. Can you find the one point at which all lines of depth meet?

Find the *horizon line.* Find the dotted vertical line. See where they meet in the center. This point on the horizon —as far as you can see—is called the vanishing point. We will refer to the vanishing point often as we draw the interior of space station 2018.

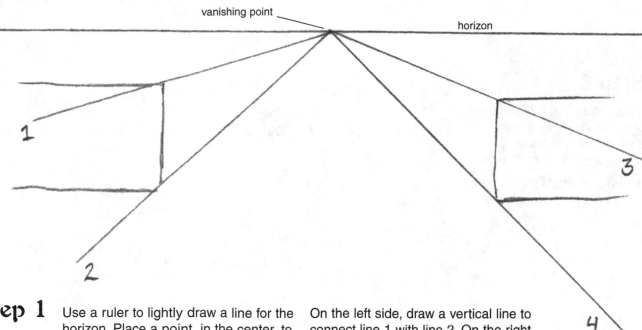

Step 1

Use a ruler to lightly draw a line for the horizon. Place a point, in the center, to represent the vanishing point. Look at the angles of lines 1 through 4. See how they meet at the vanishing point. With a ruler, draw the four lines.

On the left side, draw a vertical line to connect line 1 with line 2. On the right side, draw a vertical line to connect line 3 with line 4. Draw horizontal lines to form walls on both sides of the corridor.

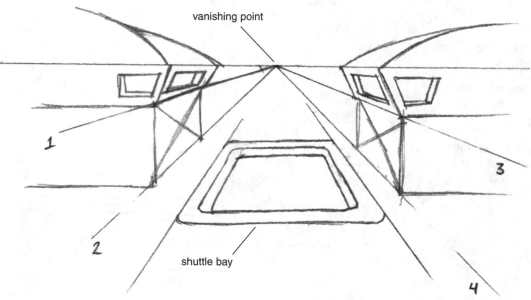

Step 2

Add cross lines on the left and right side walls. Look at the shapes above the side walls—these are for window placement. Draw shapes above—two lines, at an angle, up to the horizon and two curved lines meeting above the horizon—on the left and right side.

Next, add the shuttle bay area. Remember all lines of depth meet at the vanishing point.

Use a ruler and lightly draw guide lines for the outside of the shuttle bay. Round the corners where the horizontal and vertical lines meet. Sketch lines for the inside of the shuttle bay. Round the corners. Add an additional line—on the top and sides— to add depth to the inside of the bay.

Step 3

Look carefully at the placement of the windows, and their shapes. Add the four windows—two on each side.

Shape and shade the iron grid cross bars on the side walls.

Step 4

Let's add arches and beams for sky light windows.

First sketch the three curved lines on either side. Next, sketch the arches.

Congratulations! You have drawn the basic interior structure.

Step 5

Study the finished space station drawing on page 47. Notice the thickness of the beams, and how distant stars and planets add depth and realism to the drawing. Use the drawing on page 47 as a guide to finish your drawing of space station 2018. *Have fun!*

Chapter VI • More Ideas

Alien Settings

Use your imagination and have fun creating alien settings. Try these settings, then make up some of your own. Remember not many people have been out there YET... so anything goes!

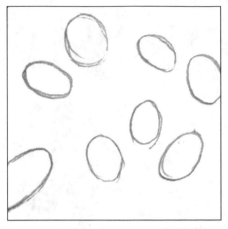

Sketch ovals to begin the Saturnian suction plants.

Sketch smaller ovals—inside the ovals—and long curvy stems.

Add thorns and shading.

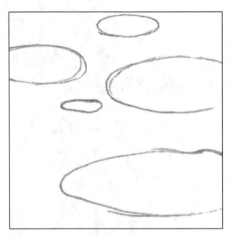

Sketch oval spheres to form the floating lily pads, unique to the Rhinegolian rain forests.

(I made up the name Rhinegolian. I have a great imagination!) Add more ovals and stems.

Shade, add a floating Rhinegolian creature, and you'll have a unique alien setting.

Begin with circles and star shapes. Add a few planets, and a ring or two around one.

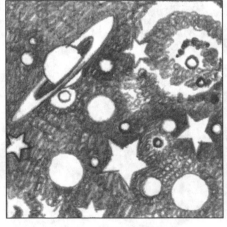

Lightly shade all around them. Leave some white space, then darken some areas to add depth

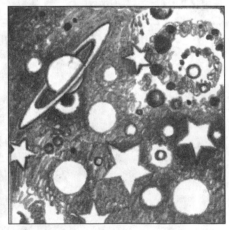

and variety. Add more shading and a few dark planets, scattered here and there.

Sketch overlapping rectangular shapes to form crystal stalagmites.

Draw lines to shape them, and connect them together.

Add shading. *The Futurenaut (p.13) landed on a crystallized planet.*

A crater landscape is easy to create. Start with randomly spaced ovals.

Sketch smaller ovals inside the original ovals. Connect the donut shapes with curved lines, to form

the crater beds. Add shading—inside and out.

To create colliding stars and great electrical blasting scenes, start with crater ovals.

Add a variety of zigzagging lines.

Remember to leave light areas. Add shading.

Symmetry

Ever notice how many things in nature have symmetry—mirrored forms on either side of a divided line?

Your face is symmetrical. A butterfly is symmetrical. A walnut is symmetrical. Bodies of animals and people are symmetrical.

See how symmetrical this character is. When his face and body are divided in half at the middle, both sides look similar.

Step 1

Let's start with the symmetrical face. Sketch a center dotted line. Sketch an oval, on each side of the center line, for the eyes. Draw the nostrils and cheeks—a small circle inside an oval, on each side.

Step 2

Look at the face shapes. Every form is duplicated on the opposite side. Draw the forehead, eyelids, jaws, nostrils holes and top lip. Sketch a large "U" to form the mouth.

Step 3

Starting at the top, form a symmetrical body around this symmetrical face. Sketch the ears, shoulders, mighty arms and fisted hands. Sketch the upper and lower body—see the small circles forming the ribs. Sketch legs, webbed feet, and tail.

Step 4

Carefully outline this beast. Shape, detail and shade.

Beautiful Beasty!

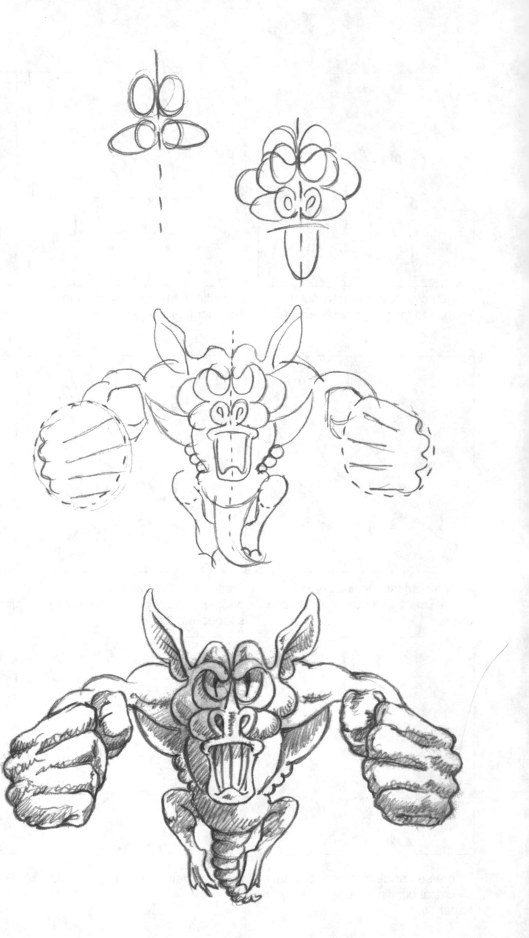

Draw Alien Fantasies

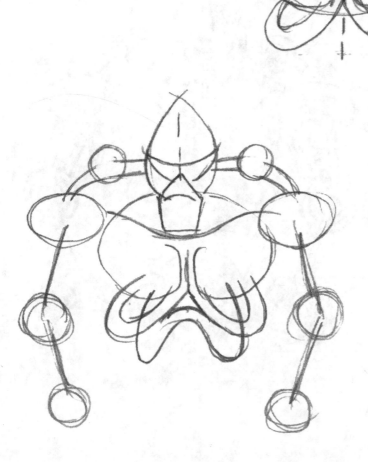

Floating Robot

The floating robot is symmetry in motion and easy to draw.

Step 1

Sketch a teardrop for the head. Sketch an oval, overlapping the teardrop, for the chest and smaller ovals on each side for the shoulders.

Step 2

Sketch a light dotted center line down the middle.

Draw a curved line, connecting the two shoulders, to form the metal collarbone.

Sketch two curved lines on each side to begin the metal ribcage.

Step 3

Sketch the triangle eyes. Just below these draw the square shaped mouth speaker.

Sketch a small circle, one on each side of the head. Add lines to connect the circles to the head.

Sketch rods and joints to form the shoulders, arms and hands. Add lines to connect the head circles and the shoulders.

Sketch a second set of ribs, under the first set.

Step 4

Add the triangle shape that divides the robot's brain. Add it now, or forever suffer the consequences of a robot who doesn't know its left side from its right!

Outline and shape the speaker mouth and tubes connecting the head to the shoulders.

Shape and thicken the shoulders, chest and upper arms. Draw three small circles in the elbow circle.

Sketch a circle for the pelvis. Add lines to complete the rib cage and connect it to the pelvis.

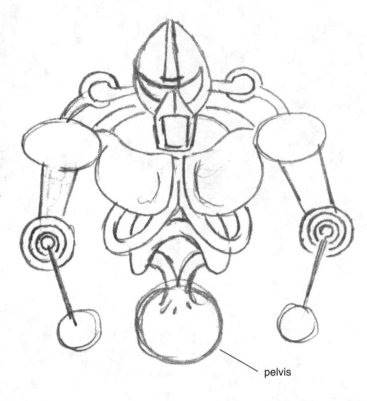

pelvis

Step 5

Look carefully at the finished drawing. See the strut shaped arms and metallic fingers. See the floating orbs. These energy globes let the floating robot levitate anytime, anyplace!

Add details and shading to finish your drawing.

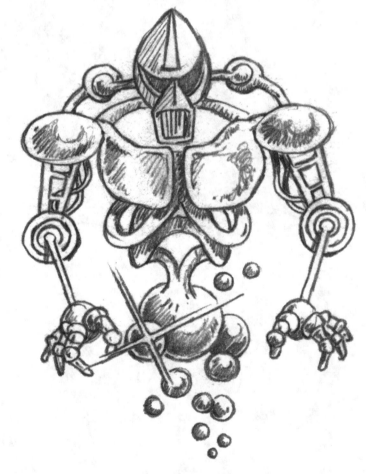

The Lil' Traveler Lands on...OZ?

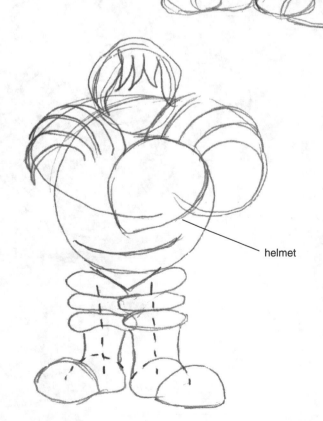

Step 1

Sketch a light oval for the Lil' Traveler's head. Sketch a half-oval, on the left side to form her curved right arm. Sketch another half-oval, on the right side to form her curved left arm. Sketch a large spiral shape, starting from the middle of the head, to form her body.

Step 2

Reshape the bottom of the body into a "V" shape. Sketch a squashed oval for the pelvis.

Add two lines and overlapping ovals to form the legs and feet.

pelvis

Step 3

Sketch squiggly lines for hair. Draw arches, on the arm lines, to form her protective suit.

Sketch the upside down tear shaped helmet. Add a curved line for her belt. Add ovals to thicken her legs. Add lines to shape the boots.

Erase guide lines and clean up any smudges.

helmet

Step 4

Draw two large, curious eyes. Add a wiggly line for her nose. Shape her smiling mouth. Shape and outline the padded arms. Add lines to form the gloves.

Draw a second line, under the belly to shape the belt.

Add square shapes for pouches on both sides of the belt.

Step 5

Add ponytails to Lil' Traveler's hair-do. Draw a dimple, or two.

LOOK at all the details!

Shape, detail and shade this happy explorer.

Space Fact...

Valentina Tereshkova became the first woman in space, when she orbited the earth 48 times in June of 1963.

Space Question...

How many years later did the first American woman go into space?

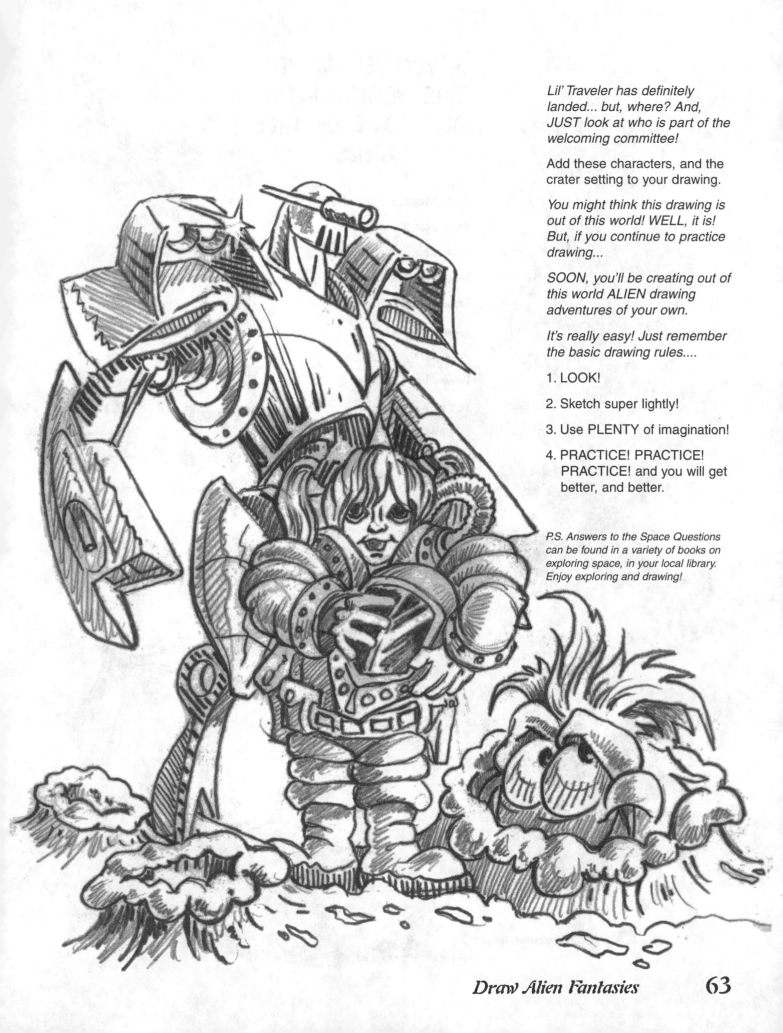

Lil' Traveler has definitely landed... but, where? And, JUST look at who is part of the welcoming committee!

Add these characters, and the crater setting to your drawing.

You might think this drawing is out of this world! WELL, it is! But, if you continue to practice drawing...

SOON, you'll be creating out of this world ALIEN drawing adventures of your own.

It's really easy! Just remember the basic drawing rules....

1. LOOK!

2. Sketch super lightly!

3. Use PLENTY of imagination!

4. PRACTICE! PRACTICE! PRACTICE! and you will get better, and better.

P.S. Answers to the Space Questions can be found in a variety of books on exploring space, in your local library. Enjoy exploring and drawing!

IF YOU'VE ENJOYED THIS BOOK, CHECK OUT SOME OF THE OTHERS!

Draw Medieval Fantasies

Draw Desert Animals

Draw Rainforest Animals

Draw Grassland Animals

Draw Ocean Animals

Draw Dinosaurs

Draw Cars

Draw Alien Fantasies

Learn To Draw 3-D

...and more to come!